THANK YOU FOR FLUSHING MY HEAD IN THE TOILET

and other rarely used expressions

A SHORT DRAMEDY BY
Jonathan Dorf

Playscripts, Inc.

The Rules in Brief

1) Do NOT perform this Play without obtaining prior permission from Playscripts, and without paying the required royalty.

2) Do NOT photocopy, scan, or otherwise duplicate any part of this book.

3) Do NOT alter the text of the Play, change a character's gender, delete any dialogue, or alter any objectionable language, unless explicitly authorized by Playscripts.

4) DO provide the required credit to the author and the required attribution to Playscripts in all programs and promotional literature associated with any performance of this Play.

For more details on these and other rules, see the opposite page.

Copyright Basics

This Play is protected by United States and international copyright law. These laws ensure that playwrights are rewarded for creating new and vital dramatic work, and protect them against theft and abuse of their work.

A play is a piece of property, fully owned by the playwright, just like a house or car. You must obtain permission to use this property, and must pay a royalty fee for the privilege — *whether or not you charge an admission fee.* Playscripts collects these required payments on behalf of the author.

Anyone who violates an author's copyright is liable as a copyright infringer under United States and international law. Playscripts and the author are entitled to institute legal action for any such infringement, which can subject the infringer to actual damages, statutory damages, and attorneys' fees. A court may impose statutory damages of up to $150,000 for willful copyright infringements. U.S. copyright law also provides for possible criminal sanctions. Visit the website of the U.S. Copyright Office (www.copyright.gov) for more information.

THE BOTTOM LINE: If you break copyright law, you are robbing a playwright and opening yourself to expensive legal action. Follow the rules, and when in doubt, ask us.

Playscripts, Inc.
325 W. 38th Street, Suite 305
New York, NY 10018

Phone: 1-866-NEW-PLAY (639-7529)
Email: info@playscripts.com
Web: www.playscripts.com

Cast of Characters

ACHILLES, early to mid-teens and a target of bullies

HELEN, female, not so different from Achilles in that she's a target

GLINDA, female, coolest of the cool

PROMETHEUS, male, even more bullied than Achilles

BULLY, male, big enough to scare his victims

ISMENE, Helen's friend

SIX SALESPEOPLE

BULLY GIRL

BULLY GIRL'S FRIEND

BULLY GIRL'S SECOND FRIEND

SEIZURE STUDENT

TRAGICOMIC INTERLUDE STUDENT

REPORTER

ONE, a popular girl

TWO, a second popular girl

THREE, a third popular girl

GIRL AT THE DESK

BLUEBIRD STUDENT

SPELLERS

TEACHER, something of a caricature

AUDIENCE KIDS

4

Cast of Character Notes

With the exception of the Teacher, all of these characters are meant to be school-age, and the Teacher is more of a caricature and is meant to be played by an actor from the ensemble.

Achilles, Helen and Glinda should not be doubled. Prometheus should not be doubled either, but he could also be one of the spellers in Scene 9. A flexible-sized ensemble of students portrays all other characters. They are also the members of the Pyramid of Popularity, the audience at the spelling bee, and create the "choral" moments in Scenes 3, 4 and 10.

Setting

The play is meant to be produced using simple, suggested settings that make use of lighting and minimal set pieces.

Production Notes

It's best for continuity if the play can be performed without blackouts between scenes unless specifically called for. It's particularly important to avoid a blackout after *Spelling Bee*, so that the audience doesn't think the play is over and start to clap.

In *Thank You for Flushing My Head in the Toilet*, a bucket could substitute for the toilet, as it did in the Springfield Academy of Arts and Academics (A3) production, or it could simply be implied, as it was at Socorro High School.

If the lines "Or straight" and "Him spreading a rumor that I have AIDS" are both said in *My Bully Buddy*, it's possible to have the same actor say them both.

The *Shopping* scene is meant to create a stereo effect, with the conversations ping-ponging back and forth between Achilles and Helen's "groups." Also, be aware that characters will often start a sentence, get interrupted and then pick up that same sentence several lines later.

In the A3 production, a video played silently to depict the events described in *Tragicomic Interlude*. It interrupted the monologue and began after the line that says "streaming it live to the web through a cell." This video is available free for use by future productions at www.thankyouforflushing.com.

In *Building a Better Bully, Part I*, "faggot" may be substituted for "freak" to make the line harsher.

In *Spelling Bee*, for full effect, put as many cast members in the audience as the production can spare.

Acknowledgments

Thank You for Flushing My Head in the toilet and other rarely used expressions premiered at the Springfield Academy of Arts and Academics, Springfield, Oregon. It was directed by Michael Fisher with the following ensemble cast:

Taylor Brennan, Kristen Buchanan, Sunrea Clayborn, Patrick Curzon, Anna Degollado, Lisa Ferschweiler, Matt Hutchings, Kodi King, Ashley McClain, Ann Marie Murray, Cherise Naranjo, Caleesha Petersen, Roth Preston, Kyla Schouten, Caitlynn Tannehill, Rihanna Walton, Raegan Weir and Kara Williams.

Special thanks also to Bonnie Carpenter and the students of Idyllwild Arts Academy, who did the first developmental reading of the play.

Thank You for Flushing My Head in the Toilet, Hagerty High School Theater Department, Oviedo, Florida (2007).

Thank You for Flushing My Head in the Toilet
AND OTHER RARELY USED EXPRESSIONS
by Jonathan Dorf

Scene 1
THANK YOU FOR FLUSHING MY HEAD IN THE TOILET

(The sound of a flushing toilet. Lights up on ACHILLES, early to mid-teens but definitely one of the less imposing boys at his school, his hair wet with the water probably dripping onto his shirt, as he stands up from having had his head flushed. A BULLY, bigger and tougher and either the same age or slightly older, is in front of him.)

ACHILLES. Thank you.

BULLY. *(Beat.)* What?

ACHILLES. Thank you.

BULLY. For what?

ACHILLES. For flushing my head in the toilet.

BULLY. What?!

ACHILLES. I loved that.

(Hugs the BULLY, dripping water on him.)

That was definitely your best one ever.

BULLY. *(Backing away:)* What are you — some kinda' freak?

(The BULLY hurries away. Beat.)

ACHILLES. That's how it goes in my mind. He shoves my head in the bowl, flushes, and I pop up, jack in the box: thank you!

(Beat.)

The problem is that in real life, I never get past choking on the bowl water. My brain is trying to say "thank you," and the rest of me is gagging, and if the toilet wasn't flushed before I — let's not even go there.

(Beat.)

Since "thank you" doesn't seem to be happening, I'm working on another strategy: vomiting. I'm optimistic about vomiting, because it's all I can do not to vomit already, so this would be like going with the flow, and even better: his legs are right there.

(Demonstrates by getting on his knees and swiveling to one side.)

It's just point and shoot. And if you knew that every time you gave me a swirly you were gonna' have to go home and change your pants, you'd think twice. It's the power of retaliatory vomiting.

(Beat.)

And that's just the beginning. They say that the best defense is a good offense, which is why I'm taking it to the next level: preemptive vomiting.

(Beat. "Four o'clock" in the next line means the location, not the time.)

Trouble at four o'clock. Fire projectiles on my mark.

(Feigns vomiting.)

We've got on 'em on the run. I repeat. The enemy is in full retreat.

(Beat.)

I hate vomiting. It's the worst feeling in the world. Almost as bad as having your head stuck in a flushing toilet.

(Exit ACHILLES.)

Scene 2
THE UNBEARABLE LATENESS OF BEING

(Morning. Before school. HELEN holds her bookbag. Her friend, ISMENE, also female, carries one as well. They're on their way out of Helen's house—which can be suggested by lighting or by a door frame or something similarly minimal—when HELEN stops.)

HELEN. Hold on—I forgot my homework.

(HELEN goes back inside. ISMENE waits. Beat. HELEN returns.)

ISMENE. 'K?

HELEN. Yeah.

(They take a few steps, but HELEN *stops again.)*

Wait. I forgot my homework.

ISMENE. But you just—

HELEN. That was math. This is English.

ISMENE. Hurry or we'll miss the bus.

*(*HELEN *goes back inside. Beat. She returns waving the missing homework. They turn to leave again, but after another few steps…)*

HELEN. Wait—sorry. I forgot my homework.

ISMENE. But—

HELEN. This is history. Mrs. Paul is my favorite teacher. There's no way I could bring all my other homework and not hers.

ISMENE. We're going to miss the bus.

HELEN. It's OK. You go. I'll just be a little late.

(The scene rewinds itself to the same starting point as before, with the two girls toting their backpacks.)

HELEN. Hold on—I forgot my wallet.

*(*HELEN *goes back inside.* ISMENE *waits. Beat.* HELEN *returns.)*

ISMENE. 'K?

HELEN. Yeah.

(They take a few steps, but HELEN *stops again.)*

Wait. I forgot my cell phone.

ISMENE. But you're not even allowed to—

HELEN. I'll want it for after. It'll just be a sec.

ISMENE. Hurry up.

*(*HELEN *goes back inside. Beat. She returns waving the missing cell phone. They turn to leave again, but after another few steps…)*

HELEN. Wait—sorry. My socks don't match.

ISMENE. But—

HELEN. Everybody'll see. I can't have everybody see me with these socks.

ISMENE. We're going to miss the bus.

HELEN. It's OK. You go. I'll just be a little late.

(Once again, the scene rewinds to the beginning: the two girls and their bookbags. They take a few steps, but HELEN stops again.)

HELEN. Wait. I forgot my lucky penny.

ISMENE. But—

(Before ISMENE can say another word, they freeze and the scene rewinds itself yet again.)

HELEN. I have to go to the bathroom.

(Before ISMENE can say a word, they're already rewinding and starting the scene over.)

I forgot to say bye to my Mom—

(HELEN starts to go back inside but doesn't get that far before they freeze and rewind.)

I forgot—

(ISMENE drops HELEN's bookbag.)

ISMENE. You can't keep being late.

(Beat.)

They probably moved on to somebody else by now.

HELEN. Just a few more days.

ISMENE. You keep bein' late you're gonna' get suspended.

HELEN. *(Beat.)* I think I forgot my...I just want to be late again today.

(Beat. ISMENE exits. Lights slowly fade on HELEN, just waiting.)

Scene 3
YOUR BULLY BUDDY

(GLINDA, *"in" in every way, appears across the stage from* HELEN.)

GLINDA. Hey.

(HELEN *keeps her head down.*)

I said "Hey."

(*This time* HELEN, *her head still down, looks discreetly around her, to see if there's anyone else around.*)

Late girl — I'm talking to you.

(HELEN *finally looks up.*)

HELEN. Sorry.

GLINDA. What are you sorry for?

HELEN. You said —

GLINDA. No wonder you're on the ignore list.

HELEN. What's the —

(GLINDA *holds up a hand for silence.*)

GLINDA. A picture is worth a thousand words.

(GLINDA *snaps her fingers, and* STUDENTS *representing a variety of social groups enter and set up the school cafeteria.*)

FIRST PYRAMID STUDENT. The Pyramid of Popularity: A Dramatic Interpretation.

(*Using tables or blocks or another creative design, the students at the top of the school food chain set themselves up at the top of the pyramid, and other students fill in the subsequent blocks as they work their way down: feel free to craft the pyramid and its components — jocks, preps, skaters, goths, nerds, etc — as best fits your school. Each new block of the pyramid pushes* HELEN *further down, until she's on the floor at its foot. At precisely that moment, the* BULLY *from*

the opening scene — or any other student, most likely male — uncere-
moniously dumps ACHILLES *on the floor, as the* PYRAMID KIDS
begin exiting.)

HELEN. Hey — where's everybody…

(The PYRAMID KIDS *are gone. Beat.)*

ACHILLES. This is my spot.

HELEN. It's the floor.

ACHILLES. Yeah?

HELEN. You don't own the floor.

ACHILLES. Possession is nine-tenths of the law.

HELEN. What is that supposed to mean?

ACHILLES. It's a common expression.

HELEN. I've never heard anybody —

ACHILLES. It's a common —

HELEN. Maybe if you didn't talk that way you wouldn't get your head flushed down the toilet.

ACHILLES. *(Beat.)* In.

HELEN. What?

ACHILLES. In. Not down. If I had my head flushed down the toilet, I wouldn't have a head anymore. It would be in the sewage system by now or part of a landfill: my head gets flushed in.

HELEN. I thought we were in the cafeteria.

(HELEN starts looking for a door.)

Where are we?

(ACHILLES gets up and starts looking as well.)

I was talking to this girl.

ACHILLES. What girl?

HELEN. I don't know. Just this girl.

ACHILLES. Did she look like a supermodel?

HELEN. What does a supermodel look like?

ACHILLES. Was she hot?

HELEN. More like tough.

ACHILLES. But in a hot kinda' way?

HELEN. She's a girl. I don't like girls.

ACHILLES. I didn't say you did.

HELEN. Some people say I do, but I don't.

ACHILLES. So why do they say it?

HELEN. *(Shrugs.)* 'Cause they can?

ACHILLES. *(Beat.)* So did she look like a supermodel? Black leather jacket, tight—

HELEN. Can you get to the point?

(HELEN continues futilely to look for a door.)

ACHILLES. I was talking to her too. She comes up to me, and she says she knows about the toilet.

(Enter GLINDA.)

And I'm like what toilet? And she says:

GLINDA. The toilet closest to the wall in the boys bathroom by the main office. The far wall. The second toilet to the right when you walk into the boys bathroom on the second floor by Mr. Doberman's math room. And the third toilet to the right. The one closest to the wall. The near wall. There must be something about standing next to a wall when you flush someone's head in the toilet. I'll have to try it.

(To herself, as if she were them:)

But Glinda, why are we here?

(HELEN searches the area where GLINDA entered, looking for a way out, but there is none.)

Why are we here in this place with no doors or windows or means of escape of any kind?

HELEN. *(Beat.)* Well...?

GLINDA. You're here because you've been recommended.

ACHILLES. For what?

GLINDA. A special program.

HELEN. *Special* special, or special retarded?

GLINDA. Remedial.

ACHILLES. But I'm ahead in all my —

GLINDA. Who are you ahead of? Most of the time I see you, you're upside down or flat on your face. How many people does that get you ahead of?

> *(Beat.)*

Don't you get tired of being the butt of every joke and —

HELEN. Those dirty looks every time I sit in the wrong seat or how when I walk by they all stop talking —

ACHILLES. Being checked into the lockers —

> *(The* CHORUS OF STUDENTS *forms gradually, with students entering and becoming lit just before they speak. The speaker should change after every line unless otherwise noted, but depending on the production, the chorus could be anywhere from a handful of actors rotating quickly to a large group.* ACHILLES *and* HELEN *could pick up lines here, but* GLINDA *should not — nor should any student who is obviously playing a bully at that moment.)*

CHORUS OF STUDENTS. The dog turd in my lunch bag.
The foot that trips me in the aisle every time I get on the bus.
Hearing about all the parties I didn't get invited to.
How they make fun of my weight.
And my height.
And my pants being too short.
And the car my parents drive.
And my skin problems.

And the way I talk.

> *(Beat.)*

The panic attacks in the middle of the night.
The text messages in the middle of the night saying "you're gonna' get it tomorrow."
Stealing my clothes while I'm in the showers at gym.
Taking my pencil.
Taking my homework so they can copy it.
Making me do their homework.
The stuff I told her about my brother going in her blog.

> *(The next three lines are optional, but recommended if they make sense for your production. They should be done together or not at all.)*

Calling me names because I'm not white.
Or Christian.
Or straight.

> *(To make this next line stronger, use "AIDS" instead of "herpes." If absolutely necessary, the line can also be cut completely.)*

Him spreading a rumor that I have herpes.
All the people I thought were my friends laughing when I got my shirt caught in the car door—pretending they didn't see me.

FINAL STUDENT. And this feeling that no matter what I do...

CHORUS OF STUDENTS. *(Delivered by a single student or by the entire chorus:)* What if it gets worse?
How long until I snap?

FINAL STUDENT. This feeling—

CHORUS OF STUDENTS. *(Delivered by a single student or by the entire chorus:)* Of being totally alone.

FINAL STUDENT. That no matter what—

ACHILLES. I don't know how much longer—

HELEN. *(Finishing his sentence:)* I can take this.

FINAL STUDENT. That it will never ever stop.

(Lights dim on the chorus of students: it's just GLINDA, ACHIL-LES and HELEN.)

GLINDA. *(Beat.)* Do you wanna eat lunch or be lunch?

(GLINDA holds out her hand to ACHILLES and HELEN. A light appears, as if it's a door, behind her. ACHILLES and HELEN step toward her. Blackout.)

Scene 4
SHOPPING

(GLINDA gives ACHILLES and HELEN a push, thrusting them into the Bully Store, then fades into the background. The Bully Store, which looks vaguely like a real store, is filled with SALESPEOPLE, all of whom can be played by teen actors. The conversations between HELEN and ACHILLES, while meant to be separate, should inter-twine sufficiently so that at times they seem like one, with the SALESPEOPLE coming at them at lightning speed, further blend-ing them together.)

FIRST SALESPERSON. Step right up.

SECOND SALESPERSON. *(Steering HELEN away from ACHILLES and into a different section of the store:)* Step right over here.

ACHILLES. *(To HELEN:)* Where are you —

FIRST SALESPERSON. *(To ACHILLES:)* You want it, I've got it!

SECOND SALESPERSON. You are in good hands, little lady.

THIRD SALESPERSON. *(Near ACHILLES:)* Mace.

ACHILLES. I don't —

HELEN. I don't have any money.

SIXTH SALESPERSON. *(Near ACHILLES:)* Pepper spray.

ACHILLES. I don't —

THIRD SALESPERSON. Knives.

FIFTH SALESPERSON. *(Near HELEN:)* No need.

HELEN. What do you sell?

THIRD SALESPERSON. Guns.

FOURTH SALESPERSON. *(Near* HELEN:*)* Everything's free here.

THIRD SALESPERSON. Free delivery on Tuesdays!

SECOND SALESPERSON. Free will.

FIRST SALESPERSON. That's on everything.

(The SALESPEOPLE *take* HELEN's *measurements as if they're fitting her for a dress.)*

THIRD SALESPERSON. But especially on bombs.

SIXTH SALESPERSON. Homemade or professionally assembled for a reasonable fee.

HELEN. Am I getting a makeover?

FOURTH SALESPERSON. Sometimes the best defense is a good offense.

THIRD SALESPERSON. Or tasers: no fuss, no muss —

FIFTH SALESPERSON. Think outside the box.

SIXTH SALESPERSON. Just enough voltage to have 'em flopping like a flounder.

ACHILLES. I don't want to hurt anybody.

FOURTH SALESPERSON. Think inside the box.

FIRST SALESPERSON. Would you like that in a bag or a box?

ACHILLES. I just want them to leave me alone!

FIRST SALESPERSON. I've got just the thing: Bully Boy's Deluxe Isolation Chamber. Guaranteed to save your face by giving you space.

SECOND SALESPERSON. I've got just the rumor.

HELEN. About me?

THIRD SALESPERSON. No one will come near you.

FOURTH SALESPERSON. Matches your eyes.

FIFTH SALESPERSON. Ruthless.

FIRST SALESPERSON. They won't touch you with a ten-foot pole.

THIRD SALESPERSON. Fifteen.

HELEN. A rumor about me?

SECOND SALESPERSON. Of course not. You're starting it.

FIRST SALESPERSON. Twenty with the ultra-deluxe model.

FOURTH SALESPERSON. One rumor with anonymous graffiti, coming right up.

SECOND SALESPERSON. Eat lunch at your own table.

HELEN. About what?

THIRD SALESPERSON. Be the only kid unpicked for teams in gym class—on purpose.

SECOND SALESPERSON. It's a rumor. What does it matter?

FIRST SALESPERSON. Be the only group of one for science labs.

ACHILLES. But I'll have no friends.

FIRST SALESPERSON. Do you have so many now?

FIRST SALESPERSON. Our design team is already making the website.

THIRD SALESPERSON. Do you have *any* now?

FOURTH SALESPERSON. And the blog—

FIFTH SALESPERSON. Oh what a blog.

FOURTH SALESPERSON. All her secrets.

HELEN. Who am I making—

(*The* FIRST *and* SECOND SALESPEOPLE *switch places as the conversation continues, carrying on as if they'd been in their new spaces all along.*)

ACHILLES. What did I ever do to them?

FIRST SALESPERSON. *(To* HELEN *this time:)* Who cares?

SECOND SALESPERSON. *(To* ACHILLES *now:)* Might just keep your head out of the toilet.

FIFTH SALESPERSON. Pictures you took on your cell phone in gym.

FIRST SALESPERSON. *(To* HELEN:*)* You'll rip her to shreds.

HELEN. I don't want to —

FIRST SALESPERSON. Don't you want to get even?

THIRD SALESPERSON. Results not guaranteed.

HELEN. I'm not like that.

FIRST SALESPERSON. Don't tell us the thought —

HELEN. I said I'm not —

SECOND SALESPERSON. *(Waves a shower cap:)* Act now —

FIRST SALESPERSON. Hadn't crossed your mind.

SECOND SALESPERSON. And we'll throw in this disposable shower cap.

HELEN. I'm not.

FIRST OR SECOND SALESPERSON. *(Responding to* HELEN's *last line, which continues the "I'm not like that" thread:)* Not yet.

> *(The* THIRD SALESPERSON *holds out the shower cap to* ACHIL-LES. *Beat as* ACHILLES *and* HELEN *push through the* SALES-PEOPLE *to get to* GLINDA.*)*

ACHILLES. *(To* GLINDA:*)* I want to go home.

HELEN. Me too.

GLINDA. Of course you do.

> *(A very long moment.)*

HELEN. Well?

GLINDA. You can go back anytime you want.

ACHILLES. Then I want to go back.

GLINDA. You just got here.

HELEN. And we want to leave.

GLINDA. We? *(To HELEN:)* Since when are you with him?

HELEN. *(Beat.)* I'm not. We just both want to go. At the same time.

GLINDA. *(To herself, but so they can hear:)* The second the man goes...

HELEN. It's got nothing to do with him.

GLINDA. Then go.

> *(Beat.)*

Just click your heels three times.

ACHILLES. *(Not buying it:)* Click our heels.

HELEN. That's the Wizard of Oz.

ACHILLES. *(Starting to look around the space:)* I'll bet there's a hidden camera.

GLINDA. There's no wizard in this story.

ACHILLES. It's probably streaming to the web, just like that kid Jason.

GLINDA. Try it if you don't believe me. But you'll wish you hadn't.

> *(Beat. ACHILLES clicks his heels once, then looks at HELEN, who watches him. She clicks her heels once. Both look at GLINDA, then HELEN clicks again. ACHILLES follows her a split-second later.)*

See you soon.

> *(ACHILLES and HELEN click their heels one last time – together – and the lights change. They're back in real time. STUDENTS swarm the stage, coming at them from all sides. HELEN gets jostled into a desk chair, which appears almost from nowhere. One student shoves a bookbag into ACHILLES's hands, while another does the same*

with a dollar bill, which the BULLY *from the bathroom – or a* NEW BULLY *– promptly takes.)*

BULLY. Thanks for the lunch money.

(HELEN gets a bully of her very own, a GIRL. *The two conversations intertwine, just like in the Bully Store.)*

BULLY GIRL. *(To* HELEN:*)* That seat is taken.

BULLY. *(To* ACHILLES:*)* Tell, and you're food.

(A TEACHER, *who could be imaginary or be played by a student actor, passes by. The* BULLY *pats* ACHILLES *on the back.)*

Oh – hi, Mr. Powers.

(Beat.)

Bye, Mr. Powers.

(The BULLY *whacks* ACHILLES *on the back or perhaps cuffs him in the back of the head. Some of the* BULLY GIRL'S FRIENDS *surround* HELEN, *who gets out of the seat she was in.)*

BULLY GIRL. Helen, congratulations. You definitely know how to get the most out of the thrift store bargain rack.

(Enter PROMETHEUS, *or* PROMEY *for short, male and young-looking, holding an appointment book and flanked by several* TOUGH-LOOKING KIDS.*)*

PROMETHEUS. Sorry, I'm getting spray-painted at one. But I could fit you in after school – say three o'clock?

BULLY GIRL'S FRIEND. Two words, Helen.

FIRST TOUGH-LOOKING KID. *(To* PROMETHEUS:*)* Works for me.

BULLY GIRL. Make up.

PROMETHEUS. Don't be late – I'm getting my shoelaces tied together at 3:30, and I have to say horrible things about my mother at 3:45…

(Sees ACHILLES:*)*

I'm so glad you're back.

BULLY GIRL. *(To* HELEN:*)* Did they name you after Helen of Troy?

BULLY GIRL'S FRIEND. No—Helen Keller.

(PROMETHEUS *hands* ACHILLES *the appointment book.*)

PROMETHEUS. They're all yours.

BULLY GIRL. Was Helen Keller a total dog?

(*Gradually, the* BULLIES *and* TOUGH-LOOKING KIDS *trap* ACHILLES, *cutting off his path no matter where he goes. The other kids see what's going on, and more and more they laugh and point at it. This goes on in pantomime during* HELEN's *exchange with the* BULLY GIRL's SECOND FRIEND, *only becoming louder once their conversation ends.*)

BULLY GIRL'S SECOND FRIEND. *("Bs" is pronounced "bees.")* Hey, Helen—sorry—they're being total Bs.

HELEN. It's all right.

BULLY GIRL'S SECOND FRIEND. You want to go to the mall with us after school?

HELEN. Uh...

BULLY GIRL'S SECOND FRIEND. We'll totally make it up to you.

(*Beat.*)

Come on—don't you want to hang out with us?

HELEN. *(Getting more comfortable with the idea:)* Yeah. OK.

BULLY GIRL'S SECOND FRIEND. Be at Walnut Grove at four. West entrance. Under the fake palm tree.

(HELEN *nods, more and more excited, as the* BULLY GIRLS *turn and walk away.*)

BULLY GIRL'S FRIEND. *(To* BULLY GIRL'S SECOND FRIEND:*)* I thought we were going to Maple Shade.

BULLY GIRL'S SECOND FRIEND. *(Putting a finger to her lips:)* Shhh...

> *(They burst into laughter, which combines with the laughter at ACHILLES, spreading like wildfire across the stage until the entire cast is laughing at ACHILLES and HELEN. All freeze, and then the SEIZURE STUDENT, male or female, unfreezes.)*

SEIZURE STUDENT. Do I have a sign painted on my head? I must. An invisible bullseye that says "get me." It's the only thing I can come up with, because —

> *(A SECOND STUDENT unfreezes just in time to interrupt.)*

SECOND STUDENT. They don't even know me.

> *(To a BULLY:)*

You don't know me. You don't know that I collect 1950s movie posters —

> *(One by one, the non-bully students unfreeze to speak. Depending on the size of the cast, the following lines – which are a Greek chorus of bullied students – may be given to a handful of students or to more than a dozen. Ideally, almost the entire cast would be unfrozen and speaking by the end. Like before, the speaker should rotate after every line. ACHILLES, HELEN, GLINDA and anyone playing a bully at the moment should not join in.)*

SERIES OF STUDENT VOICES. Or that I want to be a vet.
Or that I volunteer at a soup kitchen every other Sunday.
Or that my favorite color is blue.
That I do the New York Times crossword puzzle.
That I help out at my grandfather's store —
And I cook dinner so my Mom doesn't come home from a twelve hour day and have to work some more.

> *(Beat.)*

You don't know that I have a cat named Thurgood —
Or that my little brother is autistic.
That I have nightmares about being chased by exactly five pieces of sushi.
You don't know that my parents make me pay rent.

Or that I'm a DDR champion.

(The actor should substitute the name of a nearby prison for San Quentin in the next line.)

And my father is doing five to ten at San Quentin.
That I really do like long walks on the beach
And stuffed animals — but only bears.
That I wear long sleeve shirts because I cut.
That I want to be the next Jimi Hendrix —
Or the next Steven Spielberg —
Or the next me.
I haven't told you that I play hopscotch with my sister when she comes home from college.
Or that I do a mean Elvis impression:

(The same student, as Elvis:)

Thank you very much.

(Another student, no longer Elvis:)

That I got a gym membership for my birthday.
And last summer, I went hiking in the Andes.
Or that I don't eat lunch so you won't see me get a free one.

SEIZURE STUDENT. And that I begged my aunt to let me live with her, so I wouldn't have to go through this every day.

(Beat. All freeze again, except for the SEIZURE STUDENT.)

We haven't had these conversations.

(Beat.)

Three months ago I had a seizure. It's after school, and I'm trying to get across the front lawn to my bus. I've prepared a diagram.

(The SEIZURE STUDENT pulls out a diagram. It's a map of the front yard of the school, broken up into four or five huge chunks, each a different color like countries on a map. Through them threads a tiny sliver of white: a path.)

See these colored patches? You can't walk there — unless you're just tired of breathing.

(Beat. Illustrating using the diagram.)

Normally, it's fine. You go straight out the front doors, turn left here, turn right here, then one more left and — you gotta' watch out for the occasional floater — but other than that you're home free.

(Beat.)

Only on this day three months ago, there has been a shift. The path is gone.

(The SEIZURE STUDENT *pulls out a new diagram that reflects the shift: the path is gone, and the colored patches have taken over the entire map.)*

I think about running really fast. Maybe I can get by before they notice me, but my book bag weighs 38 pounds, 9 ounces. I put it on the scale in science. I vow to buy two of everything from now on so that I will never again have to carry my books home, but for today, I'm trapped and there's nowhere to go but down.

(Beat.)

That's it! I will go down. I take a deep breath, gliding to the bottom of the steps and strategically positioning my book bag so it won't crush me, and I let my eyes roll back in my head and my hands start to shake and then my whole body, and I fall down, twitching and even drooling. The drooling is gross and embarrassing, but it totally sells the seizure.

(Beat.)

And from then on, on the days when the path disappears, I know what I have to do.

(Beat. To ACHILLES *and* HELEN, *who unfreeze just ahead of the rest of the cast, who then unfreeze. The laughter slowly returns.)*

Need an exit? Fake it and shake it.

(Just as the laughter builds to even greater heights than before and ACHILLES *and* HELEN *seem totally trapped, they fall down into fake seizures. The laughter fades as the other students edge away uncomfortably and exit, leaving the stage dark and silent.)*

Scene 5
Tragicomic Interlude

(A STUDENT stands in a spotlight/special.)

TRAGICOMIC INTERLUDE STUDENT. Funny story: this kid at school, Jason, they mess with him all the time. No idea why. Nothing big. There's only been blood like two or three—wait—four times. But it's not like he needed a transfusion.

(Beat.)

One day last week they break his glasses. Without them, he's blind. Like walk into the door blind. How many fingers?

(Holds up two fingers in front of his eyes.)

Four?

(Waves the two fingers at an imaginary kid.)

So he barely makes it home, and his clothes are full of dirt and he's got leaf parts in his hair and when he finally gets there he's crying 'cause he can't go three steps without tripping. I only know this cause the kids who broke his glasses are following him and streaming it live to the web through a cell.

(Beat.)

Now this next part I only heard when the counselors talked to us at school, 'cause it's not like anybody could see in his house. He goes upstairs—his Dad's a doc, and so he gets all these free samples—and Jason takes this fistful of pills and swallows them. Only he's so blind he takes the wrong pills. Instead of dying, now he's an eggplant. I mean, talk about a day when you just can't do anything right.

(The light goes out on the student, and up on…)

Scene 6
BUILDING A BETTER BULLY, PART I

(GLINDA *shows* ACHILLES *into a room. Ideally, there would be multiple male teens, but there should be at least one. They seem to be practicing something, talking quietly to themselves.*)

ACHILLES. Where's Helen?

GLINDA. We've found that sometimes boys and girls learn better when they're taught separately.

(GLINDA *leads* ACHILLES *toward* PROMETHEUS, *who dunks his own head in a bucket of water.*)

ACHILLES. That's the kid from —

GLINDA. Sshhh...

PROMETHEUS. Thank you for flushing my head in the toilet.

(He dunks his own head again.)

Thank you very much.

GLINDA. With feeling this time.

ACHILLES. What is he —

GLINDA. *(Holds up a hand for silence.)* Say it like you mean it.

PROMETHEUS. Can I do one of my other ones?

(Beat. He dunks his head again — without an accent:)

Please sir, I want some more.

GLINDA. I'm not feeling it.

PROMETHEUS. But you said it was good yesterday.

GLINDA. Today it's not. Are you doing something different vocally?

PROMETHEUS. Shoot! I totally forgot the accent.

(Beat.)

How's this:

(Dunks his head again, then affects an Oliver Twist-style British accent:)

Please sir, I want some more.

GLINDA. *(Takes a moment to consider.)* You got me right here.

PROMETHEUS. And then I do this.

(He shoves his head in the bucket again. Almost like he's frolicking as he sings to the well-known children's tune:)

Rubber Ducky, you're the one. Rubber Ducky—

(Not singing:)

Is the Rubber Ducky song too much?

GLINDA. Achilles?

ACHILLES. Uh…

PROMETHEUS. If I did the Rubber Ducky song, would you think I was nuts enough that you'd leave me alone?

ACHILLES. Well…

GLINDA. Tell him what you think.

PROMETHEUS. *(Dripping water and totally cheerful:)* Yeah. I can take it.

ACHILLES. Uh…probably not.

PROMETHEUS. *(Looking ready to cry:)* Oh.

ACHILLES. *(Beat.)* But maybe if you had the Rubber Ducky in your hand…

PROMETHEUS. Like a prop.

ACHILLES. I think that just might do it.

PROMETHEUS. *(Breaking into a big smile:)* Thanks! Before you go, I've been working on a couple more.

ACHILLES. I think you got the toilet down.

(ACHILLES edges away, but PROMETHEUS grabs his arm.)

PROMETHEUS. Listen to this.

ACHILLES. Get off.

PROMETHEUS. *(Singing:)* Come on baby light my fire.

ACHILLES. I said get off.

PROMETHEUS. That's for when they set my books on fire.

(ACHILLES *tries to shake* PROMETHEUS *off, but he holds on tight.)*

ACHILLES. Stop grabbing my —

PROMETHEUS. Oh yes, my Mom is a —

ACHILLES. Get off me, freak!

(Prometheus abruptly lets go.)

GLINDA. Finally, we're getting somewhere.

ACHILLES. *(Trying to get away from* PROMETHEUS.*)* I...I didn't mean...

GLINDA. *(Following him:)* Yeah, you did. Don't worry — it's good.

ACHILLES. No.

GLINDA. They smell weakness, Achilles...

ACHILLES. It's not weakness.

GLINDA. In your eyes...

PROMETHEUS. It's OK — I get torn apart every day.

ACHILLES. It's not —

GLINDA. The way you move...

PROMETHEUS. It's what I'm for.

ACHILLES. No — you're not.

GLINDA. Even down to the tip of your heel.

ACHILLES. *(To* GLINDA:*)* I'm not weak.

GLINDA. You're so close to getting it.

ACHILLES. It's wrong.

GLINDA. It works.

(Beat.)

We're talking about survival.

(Fanfare. Enter a BULLY, possibly the one from the beginning of the play or possibly not, flanked by a REPORTER, CAMERAPERSON and any number of additional members of the press. If it's the BULLY from Scene 1, the BULLY is male – otherwise, the character could be male or female.)

REPORTER. I just want to say before we start that I am honored to have this exclusive opportunity to get your unique point of view.

BULLY. *(Pulling out a small piece of paper.)* I'm sure you are.

REPORTER. I wanted to start by –

BULLY. Thanks – I got it from here.

(Beat.)

You ask, Randy, how does it feel to run the school?

(Beat. As himself again:)

Well, we all know I run the school. I don't think that's what's on people's minds. Do you, uh…

REPORTER. Janine.

BULLY. Right.

(As if he is the REPORTER.)

People see you –

(Shoving the paper at the REPORTER and pointing at a particular spot.)

Start reading from here.

REPORTER. *(Reading from the paper:)* People see you, and yes, they see this totally cool person, but some of them get the wrong idea. Some of them even call you a bully. I know. It's shocking, but some of them have used that word. Could you tell us why they're wrong?

BULLY. That's a great question, uh…

REPORTER. Janine.

BULLY. I'm misunderstood.

(The BULLY points at another line on the paper. Beat.)

REPORTER. *(Reading from the paper:)* I know you are.

BULLY. See, people look at me, and maybe they see a shark. Yeah — like I am the Great White Shark of _____.

(The actor should say the name of his school. Beat.)

But why am I the bad guy just because I'm a shark? I'm only doing what I know how to do from watching the other sharks. I mean my Dad's always talking about buying something or other 'cause the neighbors just got it, and my coach is always pushing us to kick some butt, my teachers are like only the top four kids are getting an A. Even the wussy drama kids have their little one-act competitions so they can beat all the other wussies. So why do you hate me just 'cause I'm better at being a shark than you?

ACHILLES. Maybe we don't need to be sharks. Maybe there's —

REPORTER. Hey — this is *my* time.

BULLY. Let me close with this: stop saying I've got low self-esteem or I'm acting out 'cause my dog died or I just need love. You gave me that killer instinct. You made me the Great White. So don't cry about it now.

(The BULLY exits with his entourage. GLINDA then crosses the stage, leaving ACHILLES alone.)

Scene 7
BUILDING A BETTER BULLY, PART II

(As the lights fade on ACHILLES, who exits, the lights come up on the other side of the stage, where GLINDA escorts HELEN into the "practice" room. Some of the same students as before are there. PROMETHEUS is still dunking his head into the bucket. Lights fade on all but GLINDA, HELEN, and a GIRL AT A DESK. From

seemingly out of nowhere, a trio of WELL-DRESSED GIRLS *appear and flank* HELEN. *Elsewhere in the room, similar* GIRL *on* GIRL *scenes could be taking place in pantomime.)*

GLINDA. *(In greeting:)* One. Two. Three.

HELEN. *(Whispered:)* Who are they?

ONE. We're your clique.

TWO. Your crew.

THREE. Your backup.

HELEN. *(Whispered again:)* Don't they have names?

GLINDA. That's good. Whispering is good.

ONE. It's tight.

TWO. Phat.

THREE. It's in.

HELEN. But—

GLINDA. OK—show us what you can do.

HELEN. What am I doing?

ONE. As if.

> *(They push* HELEN *toward the* GIRL AT THE DESK. *Long silence.)*

HELEN. Hi.

GIRL AT THE DESK. Hi.

HELEN. What's that?

GIRL AT THE DESK. The Count of Monte Cristo.

HELEN. That's cool. That's—

> *(One clears her throat too loudly.)*

Weird. That's weird.

GLINDA. *(In her ear:)* You're blowing this.

HELEN. *(To* GLINDA:*)* But this is just a practice thing, right?

(*Beat.*)

It's not like it's real.

GLINDA. No. Not really.

HELEN. *(Beat. To the* GIRL AT THE DESK:*)* Your clothes are ugly.

GLINDA. Vague.

ONE. Ugly is like so five minutes ago.

TWO. Outie like the—

THREE. *(Pronounced gar-bahj.)* garbage.

GLINDA. You've got to be more subtle.

(*Louder:*)

Anybody ever seen hand-me-downs on a girl?

HELEN. So I'm just pretending.

GLINDA. Like I said, not really.

HELEN. But—

GLINDA. It's either you or her.

HELEN. *(Beat, to her "group":)* I hear there's a big party at…at…

ONE. Friday night is Blake's.

TWO. Saturday is Preston's—

THREE. But before that everybody's going down to the promenade…

HELEN. If…if you're anybody.

GLINDA. That's my girl.

HELEN. *(Loud enough so the* GIRL AT DESK *can clearly hear:)* Nobodies can't come.

ONE. Hand-me-down nobodies.

HELEN. Hand-me-down nobodies that take the bus to school can't come.

TWO. They don't count.

(The GIRL AT DESK *tries to bury herself in her book.)*

HELEN. You don't count. Except in a better off dead kind of way.

(The book burying isn't working.)

Oh—I'm sorry. Am I disturbing your concentration?

(The GIRL AT DESK *gets up and rushes off.* HELEN *waves at her.)*

Bye bye.

ONE, TWO, AND THREE. Bye bye.

GLINDA. That was beautiful.

(HELEN doesn't look all that pleased with herself. Exit ONE, TWO and THREE. Even GLINDA finally exits, leaving Helen staring on-stage as the BLUEBIRD STUDENT, male or female and the kind of person who might be a victim, enters.)

Scene 8
BLUEBIRD

(The BLUEBIRD STUDENT stands in a spotlight.)

BLUEBIRD STUDENT. There's a birdbath in my yard. In the back. We get robins, sparrows, pigeons. A lot of pigeons. Sometimes there's a cardinal. And squirrels. Yeah, I know they're not birds, but maybe the squirrels think they are. I mean there's flying squirrels—right? I've never seen one, but flying squirrels exist. Right?

(Beat.)

I like watching the birds. The real birds. The way they all kinda twitch their heads forward,

(Demonstrates a pecking motion.)

It's like they're talking to each other. Saying how's your day and how's the weather and would you like worms with that order?

Sometimes when I'm bored, I make up what they'd say. Like this one pigeon, he's complaining about his taxes to a sparrow, and the sparrow's like, "dude, maybe if you spent more time working and less time looking for handouts in the park..."

(Beat.)

I'm supposed to put water in the birdbath once a week. Today's my day. And the birds are there talking about the weather and their kids and there's a duck talking about how his cousin bought the farm and got served up in orange sauce last week. And the other birds are saying how sad that is and how sorry they are, only this one bird's not talking. He's not even in the bath. He's wet, like he was there, but he's not in there. He's on the ground under the bath, and he's trying to hop up, only he can't. There's something wrong with his left wing. He can't flap it like the right one. And he's spinning around in a circle, like he's break dancing — only he's not.

(Beat. ACHILLES enters silently and watches.)

I go over to the bath, and they all scatter when I get close. Except for the break dancing bird. It's a bluebird — I don't remember when I've ever seen a bluebird in our backyard, and now there's one spinning like a merry-go-round under the birdbath. He's beautiful. He's flapping his right wing like crazy, but the poor little guy can't go anywhere. And he's going nuts when I pick him up in my hands. I hold him real tight so he doesn't scratch me, and I've got my thumb and finger around his neck to keep him from biting. "Don't worry, little bird. I've got you." And I hold him.

(Beat.)

The phone rings in the house. I'm the only one home, but I don't move. I've got this beautiful, living thing in my hands, and that's more important than —

(Beat.)

The longer I hold him, the less he fights. He knows he's safe. I'm like the Dr. Doolittle of my backyard.

(Beat.)

And then I start to squeeze my finger and thumb together. Around his neck. Around *its* neck. Tighter and tighter. The bluebird starts going crazy. I know it can't breathe, and I don't stop. I keep going — because I can.

(HELEN continues the monologue seamlessly. She might take over completely from the BLUEBIRD STUDENT, or they might do some of the following lines together.)

HELEN. I keep going until it's— It feels good. It feels good, because for once in my life, I'm not the bird.

(For a long moment, ACHILLES and HELEN stare at each other. Enter GLINDA, staring at them both across the stage. HELEN takes a step toward GLINDA. ACHILLES doesn't move.)

ACHILLES. I...I can't.

HELEN. I'm sorry.

(She walks across the stage toward GLINDA, leaving the lights to dim on ACHILLES. Before they can go completely dim, the lights come up completely. ACHILLES is on stage.)

Scene 9
SPELLING BEE

(Several STUDENTS who are obviously the kind to get teased and bullied join ACHILLES, forming a line on stage. It's a spelling bee. PROMETHEUS could be one of the Spellers, or they could be different students. In front of them might be a podium. The COOL KIDS, now joined by HELEN, are in the audience. A TEACHER is the master of ceremonies. The FIRST SPELLER steps up.)

FIRST SPELLER. Unpopular. U-N-P-O-P-U-L-A-R. Unpopular.

(No reaction from the Teacher, so the FIRST SPELLER goes to the end of the spelling line. The SECOND SPELLER comes up.)

TEACHER. The next word is "loser."

SECOND SPELLER. Loser. L-O-S-E-R. Loser.

(The kids in the audience snicker. Somebody throws a balled-up piece of paper at the SECOND SPELLER, *who's trying to get to the relative safety of the back of the line.)*

FIRST AUDIENCE KID. Loser!

*(*ACHILLES, *third in line, approaches, looking not so much afraid as resigned, almost calm. Garbage comes his way even before he gets there. He looks to the* TEACHER, *who tries to ignore that there's anything wrong.* ACHILLES *ducks garbage while waiting for the word.)*

TEACHER. Dork.

ACHILLES. Dork.

(Beat.)

May I have a definition, please?

SECOND AUDIENCE KID. You!

(The COOL KIDS *in the audience look at* HELEN. *Beat.)*

HELEN. Dork!

ACHILLES. May I have a definition, please?

FIRST AUDIENCE KID. I'll use it in a sentence: the kid on the stage is a—

HELEN. Dork!

ALL THE AUDIENCE KIDS. DORK!

*(*ACHILLES *runs offstage, humiliated. In the audience, the kids fashion spitballs to take out the Spellers. A* THIRD SPELLER, *noticeably shaking, steps up.)*

TEACHER. Worthless.

THIRD SPELLER. Worth—

(The AUDIENCE KIDS *open fire, launching garbage and spitballs and whatever else they can throw at the spellers. The* TEACHER *puts his hand over his eyes, so as not to see the carnage.)*

FIRST AUDIENCE KID. Stupid!

SECOND AUDIENCE KID. Fashion victim!

THIRD AUDIENCE KID. You have no friends!

VARIOUS AUDIENCE KIDS. *(Depending on the size of the cast, these lines could either go to the original audience kids, or to new ones. As in the case of the earlier choruses, there should be a change in speaker after each line.)* You smell like a toilet.

Are you gonna' cry?

Toilet's gonna' cry.

Go ahead,

> *(Finishing the previous speaker's line:)*

toilet.

Everybody hates you!

HELEN. Nobody cares!

> *(In the midst of the bombardment, ACHILLES returns to the stage, wearing a long black trenchcoat. The other spellers are in full retreat, and they clear a path for ACHILLES to go straight to the podium.)*

ACHILLES. B-A-N-G.

> *(ACHILLES reaches into his coat. The others go silent, freezing in a tableau as they react to what ACHILLES is about to do.)*

You're dead.

> *(Beat. The lights should gradually shift to an almost work light quality as we move into the final scene.)*

Scene 10
HEAL

(The actor who plays ACHILLES begins as himself, not the character. Other cast members may join in as noted below, with lines assigned at the director's discretion except as noted. Ideally, HELEN, GLINDA and PROMETHEUS would speak here as well.)

ACTOR PLAYING ACHILLES. *(Delivered like spoken word or slam poetry:)* Bang bang the end my friend you're wrong.
For every Columbine, ten thousand people crying,
Suiciding,
Every one of us dying a little more each day we turn our heads and look away
When we could open our mouths and speak for every freak.

> *(At this point, other cast members may pick up the lines, or it may stay with the actor playing* ACHILLES. *Beat.)*

A push, a shove
Where's the love in words that land like houses on witches
No wizard to fix this paralysis,
This spectacular silence
That meets acts of violence,
Implying consent as spirits get bent,
Get broken with token resistance,
With mind our own business,
When we should bear witness
And stand up.
How hard is a hand up
Instead of this sleeping?
This creeping rage is killing us —
Where's the will in us to stop this mass production
Of self-destruction?

> *(The actor playing* ACHILLES *does the next three lines. Beat.)*

I started with thank you for flushing
And rushing from one crushing blow to another,
But this is your brother,

> *(Either the actor playing* ACHILLES *continues, or other cast members may join in.)*

Your sister
Caught in this twister — in danger,
No time to be strangers,
No time for that anger.

> *(Beat.)*

Heal.
This thank you is real.

(Fade to black.)

End of Play

Canned Hamlet

by Tim Kochenderfer

Comedy, 30-40 minutes
3 females, 19 males
(11-23 actors possible, gender flexible)

Life ain't easy for Hamlet. His dad's a ghost, his mother's an adulterer, and he can't make it through a soliloquy without being interrupted. *Canned Hamlet* is a one-act satirical spoof of Shakespeare's original.

15 Reasons Not To Be in a Play

by Alan Haehnel

Comedy, 30-60 minutes
14 females, 14 males, 12 either
(15-67 actors possible, gender flexible)

This is a play about not being in a play, ironically expressed through a hilarious series of monologues, duets, and ensemble scenes. From early traumas involving a glory-seeking elementary school teacher to possible disturbances in the global climate, *15 Reasons Not To Be in a Play* keeps the audience guessing just what scenario will be next.